Facts About

THE 50 STATES

Sue R. Brandt

A FIRST BOOK | REVISED EDITION
FRANKLIN WATTS
NEW YORK | LONDON | TORONTO | 1979

For permission to use material from other sources, the author and publisher wish to express their gratitude to the following: material on the origin of state names (pages 14–18), is used by permission from *Webster's Seventh New Collegiate Dictionary,* copyright 1967, and *Webster's Third New International Dictionary,* copyright 1966, by the G. & C. Merriam Company, publishers of the Merriam-Webster dictionaries.

Photographs courtesy of Wide World Photos

Library of Congress Cataloging in Publication Data

Brandt, Sue R
Facts about the 50 states.

(A First book)
Includes index.
SUMMARY: Answers questions on the geography, population, history, products, and many other aspects of the fifty states.
1. United States—Description and travel—Juvenile literature. [1. United States—Description and travel. 2. Questions and answers] I. Title.
E169.02.B73   1979   917.3′0076   79–13261
ISBN 0–531–02899–2

Contents

FOR
RONALD, A CALIFORNIAN
MICHAEL, A COLORADAN
CHARLES, A NEW YORKER
GINNY BEL, RUSSELL, AND RODDY—
ALL MISSOURIANS

Naming the States from Memory

Could you name the fifty states from memory? Most people probably could not. Yet it is not difficult to learn to do if you think of them in alphabetical order. There are——

4 "A" STATES

Alabama
Alaska
Arizona
Arkansas

NO "B" STATES

3 "C" STATES

California
Colorado
Connecticut

1 "D" STATE

Delaware

NO "E" STATES

1 "F" STATE

Florida

1 "G" STATE

Georgia

1 "H" STATE

Hawaii

4 "I" STATES

Idaho
Illinois
Indiana
Iowa

NO "J" STATES

2 "K" STATES

Kansas
Kentucky

1 "L" STATE

Louisiana

8 "M" STATES

Maine
Maryland
Massachusetts
Michigan
Minnesota
Mississippi
Missouri
Montana

8 "N" STATES
(inc. 4 "New's" and 2 "North's")

Nebraska
Nevada
New Hampshire
New Jersey
New Mexico
New York
North Carolina
North Dakota

3 "O" STATES

Ohio
Oklahoma
Oregon

1 "P" STATE

Pennsylvania

NO "Q" STATES

1 "R" STATE

Rhode Island

2 "S" STATES

South Carolina
South Dakota

2 "T" STATES

Tennessee
Texas

1 "U" STATE

Utah

2 "V" STATES

Vermont
Virginia

4 "W" STATES

Washington
West Virginia
Wisconsin
Wyoming

NO "X," "Y," OR "Z" STATES

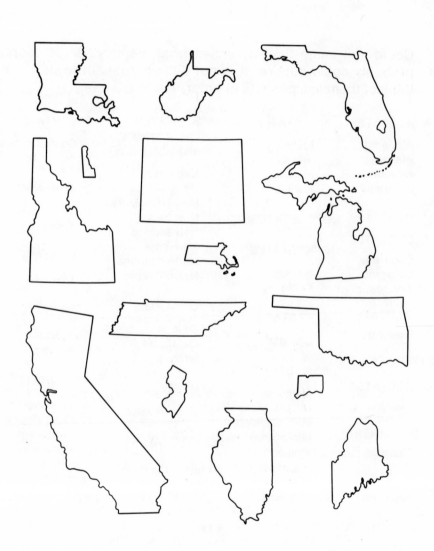

Can You Recognize These States?

The fifty states of the United States are somewhat like the members of a family. They are alike in some ways and different in others, as in size and shape. Can you recognize the states shown on the opposite page? Here are some clues:

COLORADO is an almost perfect rectangle. It is one of the few states with no boundaries formed by water.

MICHIGAN is made up of two parts. The lower part looks like a mitten.

OKLAHOMA is shaped like a stewpan, with a long, straight handle pointing to the west.

IDAHO resembles the side view of a throne, or a chair with a high back.

LOUISIANA looks like a boot with a ragged toe.

TENNESSEE is long from east to west. It resembles a sled, or maybe an anvil.

CONNECTICUT, third from the smallest state, is rectangular, except at the southwest corner.

WEST VIRGINIA has two parts called panhandles—one on the east and the other on the north.

CALIFORNIA, third from the largest state, is shaped somewhat like a human arm, with a short upper arm and a long forearm bent toward the southeast.

MAINE looks somewhat like the head of a buffalo.

FLORIDA is long from north to south, with a panhandle pointing to the west.

MASSACHUSETTS ends in a "hook" in the east.

NEW JERSEY has about the same area as Massachusetts. But New Jersey is long and narrow, with zigzags on the west and the east.

ILLINOIS resembles an arrowhead, with part of one side broken off in a straight line.

DELAWARE, second smallest of all the states, has a northern boundary that is a perfect half-circle. In shape, Delaware looks somewhat like Idaho, but Idaho is about forty times larger.

★3★

...and These?

Here are all the rest of the states except Alaska and Hawaii. How many of them can you recognize from their shape and size? The capitals are shown as extra clues. To test yourself, try to match the numbers with the list of names shown on each page. To see if you are right, check your answers against the map on pages 34 and 35.

ALABAMA
INDIANA
KANSAS
MINNESOTA
MONTANA
NEW YORK
NORTH CAROLINA
NORTH DAKOTA
OHIO
PENNSYLVANIA
RHODE ISLAND
SOUTH CAROLINA
TEXAS
VERMONT

1

2 Little Rock

★ Phoenix

3

Cheyenne ★

5

6 Des Moines

Jackson ★

4 ★ Salem

9 ★ Atlanta

Frankfort ★

7 ★ Salt Lake City

8

10 ★ Olympia

Richmond ★

15

11 ★ Pierre

13

14 Jefferson City ★

12 Madison ★

Carson City ★

16 ★ Santa Fe

17 Annapolis ★

18 Concord ★

19 Lincoln ★

ARIZONA
ARKANSAS
GEORGIA
IOWA
KENTUCKY
MARYLAND
MISSISSIPPI
MISSOURI
NEBRASKA
NEVADA
NEW HAMPSHIRE
NEW MEXICO
OREGON
SOUTH DAKOTA
UTAH
VIRGINIA
WASHINGTON
WISCONSIN
WYOMING

The Newest Members
of the Family

Alaska is so large that if a map of it were drawn to the same scale as maps of the other states, it would need a whole page all for itself. For that reason it is not shown with the states on the preceding pages. Here is a drawing that will help you understand how Alaska compares in size with the conterminous United States.*

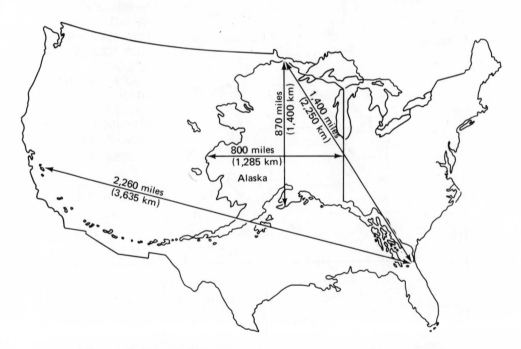

* The conterminous United States is the 48 states plus the District of Columbia, which made up the United States before Alaska gained statehood in 1959. The conterminous United States plus Alaska is called the continental United States.

If the islands that make up the state of Hawaii were drawn to the same scale as the other states, they would be so small that you could not tell very much about them. Here is a map that shows the sizes and shapes of the eight main islands. In addition, the state includes numerous scattered islets, reefs, and shoals.

ISLAND	NICKNAME	AREA SQ MI	SQ KM
Hawaii	The Big Island	4,021	10,414
Maui	The Valley Isle	728	1,886
Oahu	The Gathering Place	598	1,555
Kauai	The Garden Isle	551	1,427
Molokai	The Friendly Island	259	671
Lanai	The Pineapple Island	141	365
Niihau	The Mystery Island	72	186
Kahoolawe	(not inhabited)	45	117

N

KAUAI

Lihue

102 miles
(164 km)

NIIHAU

OAHU
Honolulu

MOLOKAI

PACIFIC OCEAN

LANAI

MAUI

KAHOOLAWE
216 miles
(348 km)

Mauna Kao
13,796 feet
(4,205 m)

Hilo

HAWAII

Mauna Loa
13,680 feet
(4,170 m)

Miles
0 20 40 60 80 100

0   40   80 120 160
Kilometers

OREGON TERRITORY TITLE ESTABLISHED IN 1846

Washington
Oregon
Idaho
Montana
North Dakota
Minnesota
Wisconsin

CEDED BY MEXICO
California 1848
Nevada
Utah
Arizona
Colorado
Wyoming
South Dakota

LOUISIANA PURCHASE
Nebraska
1803
Iowa
Kansas
Missouri

GADSDEN PURCHASE 1853
New Mexico
Oklahoma
Arkansas

TEXAS ANNEXED
Texas
1845

Louisiana
Mississippi
Alabama
Georgia
Florida

Michigan

TERRITORY OF THE

New York
Pennsylvania
Indiana
Ohio
Illinois
West Virginia
Virginia
Kentucky
D.C.
Md.

Vermont
Maine
N.H.
Mass.
R.I.
Conn.
N.J.
Del.

ORIGINAL THIRTEEN STATES
North Carolina
Tennessee
South Carolina

CEDED BY SPAIN 1819

Alaska
Purchased from Russia
1867

Hawaii
Annexed in 1959

How the United States Began— and How It Grew

The United States of America—also called the United States, the U.S.A., or sometimes "the States"—is a nation, or country, of the world. It takes its name from the fact that it is made up of states that are joined together, or united, by the Constitution to form one nation.

It began as thirteen colonies of England, spread out along the central Atlantic coast of North America. But the colonies did not come into being all at once. In fact, about 125 years passed between the founding of Virginia, the first colony, in 1607 and the founding of Georgia, the thirteenth, in 1733. More time passed—forty-three years—until the colonies joined together, rebelled against England, and declared on July 4, 1776, "That these United Colonies are, and of Right ought to be, Free and Independent States."

To gain freedom, the colonies fought the War of Independence, also called the Revolutionary War or the American Revolution. The treaty of peace ending the war was signed in 1783. By this treaty England gave up its claim to the thirteen colonies, as well as to all land east of the Mississippi River from Canada to Florida.

The map on the opposite page shows when and how the United States added more land to its territory.

This map is from *The Statistical Abstract of the United States,* published each year by the Bureau of the Census, U.S. Department of Commerce, Washington, D.C.

The Birthdays of the States

The date of the Declaration of Independence—July 4, 1776— is the official "birthday" of the United States. Each of the original thirteen states might call July 4, 1776, its birthday, too.

Why, then, is Delaware sometimes called the first state, Pennsylvania the second, and so on?

To understand why, we need to know certain facts about the Constitution of the United States.

After the War of Independence, the thirteen states were united under a form of government called the Articles of Confederation. But they soon realized that they needed a new and stronger form of national government.

In May, 1787, the states sent delegates, or representatives, to a meeting in Philadelphia called the Constitutional Convention. The delegates prepared a new form of government, which they detailed in the Constitution of the United States of America. They finished their work in September, 1787. Then a copy of the Constitution was sent to each of the thirteen states.

The people in each state chose delegates to study the Constitution and decide whether the state would ratify (approve) it. It was agreed that the Constitution would become the official form of government when nine of the thirteen states had voted to approve it. Delaware was the first to do so, and New Hampshire the ninth.

The following list shows the order in which the thirteen states ratified the Constitution:

1st	DELAWARE	December 7, 1787
2nd	PENNSYLVANIA	December 12, 1787
3rd	NEW JERSEY	December 18, 1787
4th	GEORGIA	January 2, 1788
5th	CONNECTICUT	January 9, 1788
6th	MASSACHUSETTS	February 6, 1788
7th	MARYLAND	April 28, 1788
8th	SOUTH CAROLINA	May 23, 1788
9th	NEW HAMPSHIRE	June 21, 1788
10th	VIRGINIA	June 25, 1788
11th	NEW YORK	July 26, 1788
12th	NORTH CAROLINA	November 21, 1789
13th	RHODE ISLAND	May 29, 1790

The Constitution provided that new states might be admitted by the Congress of the United States. Before they gained statehood, most of the other thirty-seven states passed through a stage when they were known as territories of the United States. The territories were organized by Congress, and the chief officers were appointed by the President and the United States Senate. When the people in a territory felt that they were ready to form a state government, they would elect delegates to prepare a state constitution. Then they would vote to decide whether they would accept the constitution and ask to be admitted to the Union.

The list on pages 12 and 13 shows when the other states were organized as separate territories, when they were admitted to the Union (their official "birthdays"), and the order in which they were admitted. The notes that follow the list explain how states that were not organized as separate territories achieved statehood.

STATE	ORGANIZED AS A TERRITORY	ADMITTED TO THE UNION	ORDER OF ADMISSION
VERMONT		March 4, 1791	14th
KENTUCKY		June 1, 1792	15th
TENNESSEE		June 1, 1796	16th
OHIO		March 1, 1803	17th
LOUISIANA	1804	April 30, 1812	18th
INDIANA	1800	December 11, 1816	19th
MISSISSIPPI	1798	December 10, 1817	20th
ILLINOIS	1809	December 3, 1818	21st
ALABAMA	1817	December 14, 1819	22nd
MAINE		March 15, 1820	23rd
MISSOURI	1812	August 10, 1821	24th
ARKANSAS	1819	June 15, 1836	25th
MICHIGAN	1805	January 26, 1837	26th
FLORIDA	1822	March 3, 1845	27th
TEXAS		December 29, 1845	28th
IOWA	1838	December 28, 1846	29th
WISCONSIN	1836	May 29, 1848	30th
CALIFORNIA		September 9, 1850	31st
MINNESOTA	1849	May 11, 1858	32nd
OREGON	1848	February 14, 1859	33rd
KANSAS	1854	January 29, 1861	34th
WEST VIRGINIA		June 20, 1863	35th
NEVADA	1861	October 31, 1864	36th
NEBRASKA	1854	March 1, 1867	37th
COLORADO	1861	August 1, 1876	38th
NORTH DAKOTA	1861	November 2, 1889	39th*
SOUTH DAKOTA	1861	November 2, 1889	40th*
MONTANA	1864	November 8, 1889	41st
WASHINGTON	1853	November 11, 1889	42nd
IDAHO	1863	July 3, 1890	43rd
WYOMING	1868	July 10, 1890	44th
UTAH	1850	January 4, 1896	45th
OKLAHOMA	1890	November 16, 1907	46th
NEW MEXICO	1850	January 6, 1912	47th
ARIZONA	1863	February 14, 1912	48th
ALASKA	1912	January 3, 1959	49th
HAWAII	1900	August 21, 1959	50th

Vermont was formed from lands claimed by both New Hampshire and New York. The dispute continued until 1777, when Vermont declared itself a free and independent republic. Finally the claims were settled, and Vermont became the fourteenth state.

Kentucky was part of Virginia until admitted as a state.

Before Tennessee became a state, it was first part of western North Carolina and then part of a large area known as the Territory South of the River Ohio.

Before Ohio became a state, it was part of a large area known as the Territory Northwest of the River Ohio.

Maine was part of Massachusetts until its admission to the Union as a separate state.

Texas was an independent country, known as the Republic of Texas, from 1836 until it was admitted as a state of the United States.

California prepared a constitution and used it to set up a government almost a year before it was admitted to the Union.

West Virginia was part of Virginia until admitted as a state.

---

* When the official papers admitting North Dakota and South Dakota were signed, the names of the two states were covered so that no one would ever know which one was admitted first.

How the States Received Their Names

About half the states have names of Indian origin. The rest were named for persons or places or in various other interesting ways.

ALABAMA: Probably from Indian words *alba ayamule,* meaning "I make a clearing" (a clearing being a piece of land cleared of trees and brush).

ALASKA: From the Aleut word *alakshak,* meaning "peninsula."

ARIZONA: Probably from the Indian word *arizonac,* meaning "few springs" or "small springs."

ARKANSAS: From Indians, the Quapaws, meaning "downstream people"; they were called "Arkansas" by French explorers.

CALIFORNIA: Probably from the name of an imaginary island in a Spanish novel of about the year 1510. Explorers gave the name to the peninsula because they thought it resembled the imaginary island called California in the novel.

COLORADO: From the Spanish word *colorado,* meaning "red" or "reddish"; the name was first given to the Colorado River by early Spanish explorers, to whom the waters looked reddish.

CONNECTICUT: Probably from the Indian words *quinni-tukq-ut,* meaning "at the long tidal river"; the name was first given to the Connecticut River, which is a tidal river, or river that flows into an ocean and is affected by the tides.

DELAWARE: From the Delaware River, named in honor of Lord Delaware (the title of Thomas West, also known as Baron De La Warr), one of the first governors of Virginia.

FLORIDA: From the Spanish words *Pascua florida,* meaning "flowery Easter." The name was chosen by the Spanish explorer Ponce de Leon because of the flowery appearance of the land and his discovery of it during the Easter season.

GEORGIA: For King George II of England.

HAWAII: Possibly from *Havaiki,* the legendary homeland of Polynesians who settled on the Hawaiian Islands.

IDAHO: Probably of Indian origin, although scholars have been unable to trace it in Indian languages.

ILLINOIS: From words in Indian languages meaning "man"; the French changed the words to Illinois.

INDIANA: From the word *Indian* plus the *-a* ending used in many geographical names.

IOWA: From the Indian word *Ayuhwa,* meaning "sleepy ones."

KANSAS: From *Kansa,* or *Kansas,* the name of a tribe of Indians who once lived in the area.

KENTUCKY: Probably related to the Indian word *kenta,* meaning "level" or "prairie," referring to the level land in the south-central part of the state.

LOUISIANA: For Louis XIV, King of France.

MAINE: Probably named by French explorers in the 1500s for Maine, an old region of France; called Maine by early New Englanders to distinguish the main, or mainland, from the many islands along the coast.

MARYLAND: Named *Terra Mariae* (Latin words meaning "Land of Maria," or "Maryland") by King Charles I of England for his wife, Queen Henrietta Maria.

MASSACHUSETTS: From Massachusetts Bay, which was named for the Massachusetts Indians, who lived around the Blue Hills near Boston; the name is made up of Indian words meaning "about the big hill."

MICHIGAN: From Lake Michigan, which takes its name from Indian words meaning "large lake."

MINNESOTA: From the Minnesota River, named from the Indian word *minisota,* meaning "white water."

MISSISSIPPI: From the Mississippi River, named from Indian words *misi,* meaning "big," and *sipi,* "river."

MISSOURI: From the Missouri River, named for an Indian people, the Missouri, meaning "owners of big canoes."

MONTANA: From the Latin word *montana,* meaning "mountainous regions."

NEBRASKA: From Indian words used as the early name of the Platte River. Later, the river received its present name and the state received the Indian name.

NEVADA: Named for the Sierra Nevada, a mountain range on the western border of the state. *Nevada* is Spanish for "snow-covered."

NEW HAMPSHIRE: From the county of Hampshire in England.

NEW JERSEY: From Jersey, an island off the coast of England.

NEW MEXICO: Named for the country of Mexico.

NEW YORK: For James, Duke of York and Albany, who received the land from his brother, King Charles II of England.

NORTH CAROLINA: From *Carolus,* the Latin form of the name Charles, in honor of King Charles I of England. (See South Carolina in this list.)

NORTH DAKOTA: From the Dakota Indians; the name means "allies."

OHIO: From the Ohio River, which probably was named from an Indian word, *oheo,* meaning "beautiful."

OKLAHOMA: From Indian words *okla humma,* or *okla homma,* meaning "red people."

OREGON: From Oregon River, an early name of the Columbia River.

PENNSYLVANIA: For Sir William Penn, father of William Penn, the founder of Pennsylvania. The last part of the name (*-sylvania*) is the Latin word for "wood" or "forest."

RHODE ISLAND: The earliest settlements were called "plantations." The first one was named Providence by its founder, Roger Williams, "in commemoration of God's merciful providence." Later, the settlements of Portsmouth and Newport were incorporated with Providence under the name Providence Plantations. The largest island in Narragansett Bay, Aquidneck, was renamed Rhode Island, possibly after the Isle of Rhodes in the Aegean Sea. In 1663 the settlements adopted what is now the official name of the state—Rhode Island and Providence Plantations.

SOUTH CAROLINA: Same as North Carolina; the two Carolinas began as a single colony, which later was divided into a northern and a southern part.

SOUTH DAKOTA: Same as North Dakota; the Dakotas began as the territory of Dakota, which was divided into two parts.

TENNESSEE: From the Tennessee River, which was named for an Indian village called Tanasi.

TEXAS: From *techas,* an Indian word meaning "allies" or "friends."

UTAH: From Yuta, the name the Ute Indians called themselves.

VERMONT: From French words meaning "green mountains."

VIRGINIA: Named after Queen Elizabeth I of England, who was known as the Virgin Queen because she was unmarried.

WASHINGTON: Named for George Washington, the first President of the United States.

WEST VIRGINIA: So named because it originally was the western part of Virginia.

WISCONSIN: Probably from the Indian word *wishkonsing,* meaning "place of the beaver."

WYOMING: From Indian words meaning "on the great plain." The name was first given to the Wyoming Valley, in eastern Pennsylvania.

How the State Capitals Were Named

Almost half of the state capitals were named in honor of persons. The others were named in various ways.

Two were named for Christopher Columbus:
COLUMBUS, Ohio, and COLUMBIA, South Carolina.

Four have names honoring Presidents of the United States:
JACKSON, Mississippi, for President Andrew Jackson.
JEFFERSON CITY, Missouri, for President Thomas Jefferson.
LINCOLN, Nebraska, for President Abraham Lincoln.
MADISON, Wisconsin, for President James Madison.

Seventeen were named for other persons:
MONTGOMERY, Alabama: For General Richard Montgomery, a hero of the Revolutionary War.
JUNEAU, Alaska: For Joe Juneau, one of the prospectors who found gold in the area in 1880.
DENVER, Colorado: For James William Denver, governor in 1858 of Kansas Territory, which included Colorado.
FRANKFORT, Kentucky: First called Frank's Ford for a pioneer, Stephen Frank, who had been killed by Indians at a ford (river crossing) in the Kentucky River.
AUGUSTA, Maine: Probably for Augusta Dearborn, daughter of Henry Dearborn, a Revolutionary War general.

ANNAPOLIS, Maryland: For Queen Anne of England.

SAINT PAUL, Minnesota: For Saint Paul to whom in 1841 Father Lucien Galtier dedicated a log church, around which a settlement, also called Saint Paul, grew.

CARSON CITY, Nevada: For Christopher (Kit) Carson, Indian scout and frontiersman.

TRENTON, New Jersey: For William Trent, a Philadelphia businessman who laid out the town.

ALBANY, New York: For James, Duke of York and Albany (later King James II of England).

RALEIGH, North Carolina: For Sir Walter Raleigh.

BISMARCK, North Dakota: For the German leader Bismarck.

HARRISBURG, Pennsylvania: For John Harris, who established a trading post at the site.

PIERRE, South Dakota: For Pierre Chouteau, a member of the family who helped to found St. Louis, Missouri, and later made a fortune trading with the Indians.

NASHVILLE, Tennessee: For Francis Nash, a Revolutionary War general.

AUSTIN, Texas: For Stephen F. Austin, a leader in Texas' struggle for independence from Mexico.

CHARLESTON, West Virginia: For Charles Clendenin; named by his son Colonel George Clendenin, a Revolutionary War soldier and owner of the land on which the settlement was built.

Three were named for other cities or towns:

LANSING, Michigan: For Lansing, a village in New York.

HELENA, Montana: For Helena, Minnesota.

MONTPELIER, Vermont: Probably for Montpellier, France.

Two capitals were named for their states:
INDIANAPOLIS, Indiana, and OKLAHOMA CITY, Oklahoma.

Four are namesakes of cities or towns in England:
HARTFORD, Connecticut; DOVER, Delaware; BOSTON, Massachusetts; and RICHMOND, Virginia.

Four capitals take their name from physical features:
LITTLE ROCK, Arkansas: From a rocky formation on the bank of the Arkansas River.
SPRINGFIELD, Illinois: Probably from a creek called Spring Creek on land where the settlement was built.
SALT LAKE CITY, Utah: From Great Salt Lake.
OLYMPIA, Washington: From the Olympic Mountains.

Eight capitals have Indian, French, or Spanish names:
SACRAMENTO, California: From *Sacramento,* a Spanish word meaning "the Blessed Sacrament."
TALLAHASSEE, Florida: From an Indian word meaning "old field" or "old town."
BOISE, Idaho: Named by French Canadians, who, after journeying through treeless country, are said to have exclaimed *"Les Bois!"* ("The woods!" or "The trees!") when they saw trees in the vicinity of the present city.
DES MOINES, Iowa: From the Des Moines River, which was probably named for an Indian tribe called Moingouena. French explorers called the river Rivière des Moingouenas, and then Rivière des Moings.
TOPEKA, Kansas: From an Indian word meaning "a good place to dig potatoes, or roots."
BATON ROUGE, Louisiana: From a red post or stick (*ba-*

ton rouge, in French) that was used to mark the boundary between the hunting grounds of two Indian tribes.

SANTA FE, New Mexico: A shortened form of the original Spanish name *La Villa Real de la Santa Fe de San Francisco de Asis* ("The Royal City of the Holy Faith of Saint Francis of Assisi").

CHEYENNE, Wyoming: For the Cheyenne Indians.

Three capitals were named for an idea:

CONCORD, New Hampshire: For the idea of concord (meaning "state of agreement, or harmony").

SALEM, Oregon: From the Hebrew word *shalom* (which means "well-being" or "peace").

PROVIDENCE, Rhode Island: Named in commemoration of "God's merciful providence" ("providence" meaning "divine guidance or care").

The rest got their names in these ways:

PHOENIX, Arizona: From the mythical bird the phoenix. Early settlers founded the city in the 1860s on lands where the prehistoric Hohokam Indians had built irrigation canals to water their crops. The settlers rebuilt some of the canals and predicted that a new city would arise "phoenixlike" where ancient Indian pueblos once stood. (According to mythology, the phoenix caused itself to be destroyed by fire and then arose from its ashes more beautiful and youthful than ever before.)

ATLANTA, Georgia: From the word "Atlantic" in the name of the Western and Atlantic Railroad; the city was the southeastern terminus of the railroad.

HONOLULU, Hawaii: The name is Hawaiian for "sheltered bay."

The Area of the States

The states are listed below in the order of their size (area), so that you can compare them easily. For example, which states would you say are medium-sized? Which states have about the same area? Alaska is how many times larger than Rhode Island?

RANK		AREA *	
		SQ MI	SQ KM
1	ALASKA	586,412	1,518,807
2	TEXAS	267,338	692,405
3	CALIFORNIA	158,693	411,015
4	MONTANA	147,138	381,087
5	NEW MEXICO	121,666	315,115
6	ARIZONA	113,909	295,024
7	NEVADA	110,540	286,299
8	COLORADO	104,247	270,000
9	WYOMING	97,914	253,597
10	OREGON	96,981	251,181
11	UTAH	84,916	219,932
12	MINNESOTA	84,068	217,736
13	IDAHO	83,557	216,413
14	KANSAS	82,264	213,064
15	NEBRASKA	77,227	200,018
16	SOUTH DAKOTA	77,047	199,552
17	NORTH DAKOTA	70,665	183,022
18	OKLAHOMA	69,919	181,090
19	MISSOURI	69,686	180,487
20	WASHINGTON	68,192	176,617
21	GEORGIA	58,876	152,489

RANK		AREA *	
		SQ MI	SQ KM
22	FLORIDA	58,560	151,670
23	MICHIGAN	58,216	150,779
24	ILLINOIS	56,400	146,076
25	IOWA	56,290	145,791
26	WISCONSIN	56,154	145,439
27	ARKANSAS	53,104	137,539
28	NORTH CAROLINA	52,586	136,198
29	ALABAMA	51,609	133,667
30	NEW YORK	49,576	128,402
31	LOUISIANA	48,523	125,675
32	MISSISSIPPI	47,716	123,584
33	PENNSYLVANIA	45,333	117,412
34	TENNESSEE	42,244	109,412
35	OHIO	41,222	106,765
36	VIRGINIA	40,817	105,716
37	KENTUCKY	40,395	104,623
38	INDIANA	36,291	93,994
39	MAINE	33,215	86,207
40	SOUTH CAROLINA	31,055	80,432
41	WEST VIRGINIA	24,181	62,629
42	MARYLAND	10,577	27,394
43	VERMONT	9,609	24,887
44	NEW HAMPSHIRE	9,304	24,097
45	MASSACHUSETTS	8,257	21,386
46	NEW JERSEY	7,836	20,295
47	HAWAII	6,450	16,706
48	CONNECTICUT	5,009	12,973
49	DELAWARE	2,057	5,328
50	RHODE ISLAND	1,214	3,144

Total area of the United States: 3,615,123 square miles
(9,363,166 sq km).

* All the area figures on pages 23 and 24 are from The Statistical Abstract of the United States.

The Population

In what way was November 20, 1967, an important date in the history of the United States?

At 11:00 A.M. on that date, a mechanism in Washington, D.C., called the Census Clock, showed that the population of the United States had reached 200 million.

In what year did the population reach 100 million?

It reached that number in 1915.

How many years did it take the nation to reach its first 100 million?

It took 308 years (from 1607 until 1915).

How many years did it take to reach the second 100 million?

Only fifty-two years (from 1915 to 1967).

Will the nation have 300 million people in another fifty years?

Most scientists do not think so, because the growth rate is now much slower than it was in the years 1915–1967.

Does the Census Clock give an exact count of the population?

No, but it is as accurate as scientists can make it. They set the dials on the clock according to recent average number of births, number of deaths, and number of persons leaving and entering the country. The mechanism of the clock balances all these figures and shows the net gain. A dial keeps track of the ever-changing total number. The clock is only one of various ways of estimating the population between the years when an official count is made.

How is the most exact count possible made?
The United States Bureau of the Census makes a count, called the census. The first census was taken in 1790, and there has been an official census every ten years since then—in 1800, 1810, 1820, and so on. The following table shows how the population of the United States has increased from time to time:

CENSUS YEAR	POPULATION	CENSUS YEAR	POPULATION
1790	3,929,214	1900	75,994,575
1800	5,308,483	1950	150,697,361
1850	23,191,876	1970	203,235,298

The list on pages 27 and 28 shows each state's estimated population (rounded to the nearest thousand) and its rank in 1978, when the estimated population of the whole country was about 218,000,000. This arrangement makes it easy for you to see how each state compares with the others in population. You can also tell something about the parts of the country that have the most people, and you can compare each state's rank in population with its rank in area (see the list on pages 23 and 24). Here are some questions that you might answer:

Which ones of the ten states that are largest in population are located along (or near) the Atlantic coast?
Which one among the first ten in population is along the Pacific coast?

Which ones of the first ten in population are along the Great Lakes?

How many of the states that rank from eleventh to twentieth in population are along the Atlantic coast (including the Gulf of Mexico) or along the Great Lakes?

States that are medium-sized in population have about how many people?

Which states are among the first ten both in population and in area?

Which ones are among the first ten in population but among the last ten in area?

Which states are among the last ten both in population and in area?

The District of Columbia had about 690,000 people. Where would it rank if it were placed in the list with the states?

RANK		POPULATION *
1	CALIFORNIA	22,083,000
2	NEW YORK	17,860,000
3	TEXAS	12,954,000
4	PENNSYLVANIA	11,783,000
5	ILLINOIS	11,273,000
6	OHIO	10,711,000
7	MICHIGAN	9,141,000
8	FLORIDA	8,506,000
9	NEW JERSEY	7,327,000
10	MASSACHUSETTS	5,781,000
11	NORTH CAROLINA	5,560,000
12	INDIANA	5,339,000
13	VIRGINIA	5,177,000
14	GEORGIA	5,083,000
15	MISSOURI	4,815,000
16	WISCONSIN	4,673,000
17	TENNESSEE	4,334,000
18	MARYLAND	4,149,000
19	MINNESOTA	3,987,000

RANK		POPULATION *
20	LOUISIANA	3,974,000
21	ALABAMA	3,712,000
22	WASHINGTON	3,684,000
23	KENTUCKY	3,473,000
24	CONNECTICUT	3,111,000
25	SOUTH CAROLINA	2,894,000
26	IOWA	2,883,000
27	OKLAHOMA	2,834,000
28	COLORADO	2,643,000
29	MISSISSIPPI	2,404,000
30	OREGON	2,402,000
31	KANSAS	2,340,000
32	ARIZONA	2,321,000
33	ARKANSAS	2,159,000
34	WEST VIRGINIA	1,873,000
35	NEBRASKA	1,566,000
36	UTAH	1,287,000
37	NEW MEXICO	1,200,000
38	MAINE	1,092,000
39	RHODE ISLAND	935,000
40	HAWAII	901,000
41	IDAHO	870,000
42	NEW HAMPSHIRE	861,000
43	MONTANA	764,000
44	SOUTH DAKOTA	691,000
45	NORTH DAKOTA	658,000
46	NEVADA	642,000
47	DELAWARE	582,000
48	VERMONT	486,000
49	WYOMING	414,000
50	ALASKA	406,000

* You will understand that population figures are always changing. As a state gains or loses in population, it may move up or down in rank. To find the latest facts about the population of each state and its rank, look in *The Statistical Abstract of the United States* or in an almanac such as *The World Almanac and Book of Facts*. New editions of these books are published each year, and they give many interesting facts about population.

The District of Columbia

The initials "D.C." in the name of the national capital, Washington, D.C., stand for "District of Columbia." The District is situated on the Potomac River, on land that once was part of the state of Maryland. Because the city of Washington covers the whole area, the names "Washington, D.C." and "District of Columbia" actually have the same meaning.

In the beginning the District included 100 square miles (about 260 sq km) given to the federal government by Maryland and Virginia in 1791. But Virginia's part was returned in 1846. The area is now 67 square miles (174 sq km).

Washington, D.C., is a federal district (an area set apart as the seat of the United States government), not a state or a part of any state. Actually, it is two cities in one. It is the federal city, with government buildings, parks, and monuments. It is also, like any other city, the home of a large number of people. About seventy percent of the residents are black.

For more than one hundred years, the Congress of the United States appointed officials to govern the city. But since 1974, Washington, D.C., has had self-government. The people elect a mayor, who is the chief executive officer, and a thirteen-member council, which makes the laws. They also elect members of thirty-six advisory neighborhood commissions, and an independent eleven-member board of education. In addition, the people elect a delegate to the U.S. House of Representatives. The delegate takes part in the work of the House but does not have a vote.

More than half of the people work in offices of the federal government. Many others have jobs in the tourist industry.

How the States Are Governed

All the states have about the same form of government. All have constitutions, much like the Constitution of the United States, which divide the powers of government into three branches.

The legislative branch legislates (makes the laws).

The executive branch executes (carries out) the laws.

The judicial branch, which is made up of a system of courts, judges questions about the laws.

The head of the executive branch of the national government is the President. The head in each state is the governor.

The legislative branch of the national government is the Congress of the United States. It is made up of two bodies, or chambers, called the Senate and the House of Representatives. In all the states except one (Nebraska), the legislative branch also is made up of two bodies.

All the states call this branch by the general name "legislature." Twenty-seven use "Legislature" as the official name, nineteen use "General Assembly," two use "Legislative Assembly," and two use "General Court."

Nebraska has a unicameral legislature—that is, a legislature of only one body, or chamber. All the other states, like the national government, have bicameral law-making bodies. (The prefix *uni-* means "one," and the prefix *bi-* means "two.") All of the states call one body the Senate, and most of them call the other body the House of Representatives.

Each state, like the nation, has a capital and a capitol. These words sometimes are confused, but they should not be.

Capital (spelled with *-tal* as the last syllable) means "city that is the seat of government."

Capitol (spelled with *-tol* as the last syllable) means "the building where the legislative branch of government meets."

In most states—but not all—the official name of the capitol is "State Capitol." Most of the capitols are stately buildings with domes, somewhat like the Capitol of the United States in the national capital, Washington, D.C.

The Geography
of the States

In land area the United States is the fourth largest country in the world. Only the Soviet Union, Canada, and China are larger. Forty-eight of the fifty states lie in the middle of the North American continent. They stretch from the Atlantic Ocean on the east to the Pacific Ocean on the west, a distance of nearly 3,000 miles (4,800 km). The north-south distance—from the Canadian border to Mexico and the Gulf of Mexico—is about half as great. With Alaska and Hawaii, the United States extends far into the Pacific.

How can we describe the huge land area of the forty-eight states? The map on pages 34 and 35 shows the main features. These are two great mountain systems—the Appalachians in the east and the Rocky Mountains in the west—with a broad lowland stretching out between them. Of course, there are many other landforms besides these. A low coastal plain extends along the Atlantic Ocean and the Gulf of Mexico. And there is another main mountain rib west of the Rockies. It is made up of the Sierra Nevada and the Cascade Range.

To have a closer look at the land in its many forms, let us board a low-flying plane on the Atlantic coast near Richmond, Virginia, and fly westward across the midsection of the country. We shall have a magical wide-angle viewer, so that we can see far and wide.

As we take off over the coastal plain, we look to the north. The view in that direction helps us understand the meaning of the word "megalopolis"—a very large urban, or city, area.

We see a seemingly endless city spread out along the coast. In this crowded megalopolis, we pick out Washington, D.C., Baltimore, Philadelphia, New York (the most crowded of them all), and Boston.

South of Richmond, the view is quite different. We see cities, of course. But beaches, swamps, and sandy offshore islands catch our eye—all the way to the southern tip of Florida and then along the coast of the Gulf of Mexico.

When we turn to the scene ahead, we are nearing the Appalachians. Quickly we look to the northeast to see where this mountain system begins (in Maine) and then to the southwest to see where it ends (in Alabama). We wish we could explore the many forested ranges, follow the rushing rivers, and stand by the sparkling lakes and waterfalls. We could do this if we packed our knapsacks someday and set out along the Appalachian Trail—a footpath for hikers that the National Park Service has marked out from one end of the Appalachians to the other. Directly below, we see where coal is dug from these mountains, especially in West Virginia and Kentucky. And we look for Cumberland Gap, the pass through the mountains where, in 1775, Daniel Boone helped carve out a road that pioneers could follow westward. The Appalachians are not high. But before that time, they served as a wall that kept settlers on the eastern side of the mountains.

Looking to the north, we see the Ohio River, flowing westward. North of the river, beginning in the state of Ohio, is the Central Lowland, which stretches as far as Kansas. This is prairie country. Once it was a vast sea of grass that grew taller than the pioneers' wagon wheels. Today it is a land where tall corn grows, along with many other crops. We see big cities, too, especially along the Great Lakes. Chicago, spreading outward from the southern tip of Lake Michigan, is the giant among them.

The United States

South of Ohio and the Appalachians are the states that once made up the cotton-growing South. Today the states in that region grow many crops besides cotton. They are part of what is now called the Sun Belt. It extends all the way across the country, from the Carolinas and Florida to California. Industries are booming there, and cities are growing. Many people from the colder northern parts of the country have been going to the Sun Belt to live and work.

Looking ahead again, we see a great river—the Mississippi—winding southward to the Gulf of Mexico. Directly below, the Ohio flows into the Mississippi. We look quickly to the north and then to the south to see where two rivers flowing from the west—the Missouri and the Arkansas—join the Mississippi in this area. As we cross the state of Missouri, we look southward for a glimpse of the Ozark Mountains and northward for a view of Iowa's rich farmlands and Minnesota's and Wisconsin's beautiful lakes and forests.

The scene below changes quickly. The land is flat and almost treeless. This is the Great Plains, extending from the Dakotas to Texas. Once it was a grassland where buffalo roamed. Now it is a land of wheat and cattle. But farmers here must be very careful to farm in ways that conserve the soil. In the 1930s this region was called the Dust Bowl. The natural grasses that held the soil together had been plowed up, and the soil was loose and crumbly. A long period of dry weather came, and wind blew tons of topsoil away. Many families left their ruined farms.

The land in eastern Colorado is flat, but we see the Rocky Mountains looming ahead. We would need a very wide view to see from one end of the Rockies to the other. They extend from New Mexico to the Canadian border, continue through Canada, and turn westward into Alaska north of the Arctic Circle. There they are called the Brooks Range. The highest peaks and ridges of the Rockies form an imaginary line called the Continental Divide. Rivers that begin west of that line flow westward to the Pacific, and those that begin to the east flow eastward.

To the north and south, we see a bewildering maze of peaks and gorges. Some parts are forested, dotted with beautiful lakes, and cut by rushing rivers. Others seem dry and bare of vegetation. Those mountains have valuable deposits of gold, silver, copper, coal, and other minerals. We look for some of the famous old mining towns, as well as for some of the equally well-known ski resorts of today. We do not wonder that the Rockies are a popular year-round vacationland.

As we speed westward, we look down upon a region of high plateaus and short, rugged mountain ranges separated by desert basins. The plateaus are cut by deep gorges. We have been keeping an eye on the Colorado River. And now, to the south, we see the work that it has done in carving the incredible Grand Canyon in northern Arizona. In this dry country we look for another famous spot, the deep desert valley in eastern California called Death Valley.

Again, mountains come into view. These are the Sierra Nevada (the name is Spanish for "snowy mountain range"). To the south is Mount Whitney, the highest point in the United States outside Alaska. Strangely enough, Mount Whitney is quite close to Death Valley, the lowest point in the country. The Sierras remind us of gold because it was gold in the Sierras that brought the first rush of settlers to California. We look to the north for a view of the Cascade Range in Oregon and Washington. The peaks there were built by volcanoes. So were the peaks of the Aleutian Range in Alaska. And all the islands of Hawaii are the tops of volcanic mountains.

Now we are passing over the fertile Central Valley of California. There and in the irrigated Imperial Valley to the south,

MUD HILLS IN
DEATH VALLEY, CALIFORNIA

people are busy harvesting huge quantities of fruits, vegetables, and other foods that will find their way to dinner tables all over the country. Ahead is San Francisco, on San Francisco Bay. Our journey ends there, at the city many people want most to visit.

Here are some interesting "highest," "lowests," and "mosts" in the fifty states:

NORTHERNMOST POINT: Point Barrow, Alaska.

SOUTHERNMOST POINT: Ka Lae (South Cape), island of Hawaii (state of Hawaii).

EASTERNMOST POINT: West Quoddy Head, Maine.

WESTERNMOST POINT: Cape Wrangell, Attu Island (one of the Aleutian Islands), Alaska.

HIGHEST POINT: Mount McKinley, Alaska—20,320 feet (6,198 m) above sea level.

LOWEST POINT: Death Valley, California—282 feet (86 m) below sea level.

DEEPEST GORGE: Hells Canyon of the Snake River, Idaho—7,900 feet (2,400 m).

HIGHEST TEMPERATURE EVER RECORDED: 134°Fahrenheit (56.7 °Celsius), Death Valley, California.

LOWEST TEMPERATURE EVER RECORDED: –79.8°Fahrenheit (–62.1°Celsius), Prospect Creek Camp, Alaska.

WETTEST PLACE: Mount Waialeale, on the island of Kauai (state of Hawaii)—average yearly rainfall, 460 inches (11,684 mm).

STRONGEST SURFACE WIND EVER RECORDED: 231 miles (372 km) per hour, Mount Washington, New Hampshire.

STATES SURROUNDED BY THE MOST OTHER STATES: Missouri and Tennessee, each surrounded by eight other states.

A PLACE WHERE YOU COULD STAND IN FOUR STATES ALL AT ONCE: The "Four Corners" of Utah, Colorado, New Mexico, and Arizona—the only place where the corners of four states touch.

Conserving the Wonders
of the Fifty States

What is the greatest natural wonder in the fifty states? Some people would say that the Grand Canyon of the Colorado River in Arizona is the most impressive and awe-inspiring. Others might choose Carlsbad Caverns in New Mexico, a great glacier in Alaska, or fiery Kilauea Crater on the island of Hawaii. Still others would mention a grove of giant sequoias in California, the seashore of Cape Cod in Massachusetts, or the mysterious, swampy wilderness of the Everglades in Florida.

Today these and many other places of natural beauty or historic or scientific interest are parts of national areas. These areas belong to all the people of the United States. They are protected and managed for the people by agencies of the federal government. These areas now number in the hundreds, and the list is ever growing. They are classified according to kinds, such as national parks, forests, seashores, recreation areas, wild rivers, wildernesses, monuments, parkways, trails, and historic places. Besides all these, there are many national wildlife refuges. Each state also has a system of state areas, classified in much the same way as the national areas.

For our present system of national areas, we can thank a group of conservationists and naturalists of the late 1800s and early 1900s. They were concerned about the waste and destruction of our natural resources—forests, soil, water, grasslands, minerals, wildlife, and places of natural beauty.

THE GRAND CANYON, ARIZONA

The Indians can be called the first conservationists in North America. They took from the land only what they needed to live, and they wasted nothing. When settlers came from Europe, they found a land of seemingly endless resources. And they used those resources to the fullest. By the late 1800s, the country was on the way to becoming an industrial giant. Forests had been cut down. Parts of the countryside were scarred by mining. Rivers had been dammed for waterpower or polluted by wastes. Grasslands had been plowed up. Many wild creatures were in danger of disappearing because of uncontrolled killing or because their natural homes had been destroyed.

It was high time to act, the conservationists said, so that future generations would have natural resources to use and places of natural beauty to enjoy. Yellowstone National Park, established in 1872, was the first national park in the United States, as well as in the world. The first national forest reserve (national forest) was set aside in Wyoming in 1891.

Do you know something (or maybe quite a bit) about your state's system of parks, forests, and other areas—and about the national areas, too? It is easy to get information. The department of parks in almost every state has available folders and bulletins telling about both state and national areas. State highway departments issue colorful maps showing where these places are and how to reach them. To anyone who asks, the National Park and National Forest services send descriptions of all the areas they manage, along with information about places to camp, hike, fish, and ski.

The work of conserving our resources—including our natural wonders—has not yet been completed. When you look around you, you see that the need to conserve resources and clean up our environment is greater than ever before. Each of us can help in this effort.

What the States Produce

When we think of what the states produce, we usually think of three main kinds of goods—agricultural (farm) products, minerals, and manufactured goods. Each state produces a share of each of these. But some states are known especially for farm products, others for minerals or manufacturing, and still others rank high in more than one kind of goods.

The nation's farms supply our food, as well as important raw materials (cotton, wool, and leather) from which our clothing is made. What a state produces depends on its geography, especially soils and climate, as well as on what products people need or want. As for food, most people think first of supplying themselves with bread and cereals (which come from wheat, corn, and other grains), meat (beef from cattle and pork from hogs), milk and other dairy products, eggs and poultry (especially chicken), vegetables, and fruits.

The states in the Central Lowland—from Ohio to eastern Kansas and Nebraska—make up one of the world's largest and richest agricultural regions. These states have deep, fertile soil, generally level land, and the kind of climate (warm, humid summers) in which corn grows best. They produce vast quantities of corn and other crops, as well as hogs and cattle. The states in the Great Plains are famous for wheat and cattle. They have the kind of soil and climate in which wheat thrives, as well as grasslands for pasturing cattle. Yet California, with its mountains and deserts, usually ranks first among the states in the dollar value of agricultural products sold each year. California has fertile valleys and a mild cli-

HARVESTING WHEAT ON A KANSAS FARM

mate in which field crops, vegetables, and fruits can be grown the year round. Huge irrigation systems provide moisture.

The following list shows the products that usually rank highest in value and the states that are the leading producers.*

CATTLE: Texas, Iowa, Nebraska, Kansas
DAIRY PRODUCTS: Wisconsin, California, New York, Minnesota
CORN: Illinois, Iowa, Indiana, Nebraska
SOYBEANS: Illinois, Iowa, Indiana, Ohio
HOGS: Iowa, Illinois, Indiana, Minnesota
WHEAT: Kansas, North Dakota, Washington, Montana
COTTON: Texas, California, Mississippi, Arizona
EGGS: California, Georgia, Arkansas, North Carolina
BROILER CHICKENS: Arkansas, Georgia, Alabama, North Carolina

Much of our food and some of our clothing come from materials on the surface of the earth. Trees, also on the surface, supply lumber for houses and furniture, and wood pulp for paper. But many other important products—everything made of metal, for example—come from materials beneath the earth's surface. These materials are called minerals. They are of three kinds—metals, or metallic minerals (such as iron ore, copper, silver), mineral fuels (coal, natural gas, petroleum) and nonmetallic minerals (salt, sulfur, stone, sand and gravel, and many others).

---

* Facts and figures about what each state produces, how much, and where it ranks among the fifty states—like population figures—change from year to year. To find the latest statistics (facts and figures), look in *The Statistical Abstract of the United States.* Most libraries have copies of this important and useful book, which is published each year. It contains information (mostly in the form of tables) about almost anything you could think of—population of the states and their cities and metropolitan areas, geography (especially area, climate, and highest and lowest points), education, transportation, communications, forests, fisheries, agriculture, mining, manufacturing, and much more.

What a state produces depends on what minerals are beneath its surface. Mineral production also depends on what minerals are in demand. Recent years have brought an ever-increasing demand for the energy supplied by petroleum and natural gas. These mineral fuels, along with coal, also provide the chemicals from which plastics, synthetic fibers, fertilizers, and scores of other products are made. Concrete (made from cement and sand and gravel) also is in great demand for use in buildings and for paving streets and roads.

Could you guess which ones of the many minerals produced each year rank highest in value—and which states are among the leading producers? The following list gives the answers.

PETROLEUM: Texas, Louisiana, California, Oklahoma
COAL: Kentucky, West Virginia, Pennsylvania, Illinois
NATURAL GAS: Texas, Louisiana, Oklahoma, New Mexico
CEMENT: California, Texas, Pennsylvania, Michigan
COPPER: Arizona, Utah, New Mexico, Montana
STONE: Pennsylvania, Illinois, Texas, Missouri
IRON ORE: Minnesota, Michigan, California, Wyoming
SAND AND GRAVEL: California, Alaska, Texas, Michigan

Today more than 300,000 factories in the fifty states turn out some 10,000 different kinds of manufactured products—from ice cream and sneakers to bicycles and huge jetliners. One group of products that rank high in value is machinery. Without machines of many kinds, farmers and workers in mines and oil fields could not produce the raw materials that factories need. And factories could not operate without the many kinds of machines used to make products. Other groups of manufactured goods that rank high in value are foods (canned, frozen, and processed in other ways), chemicals and chemical products, transportation equipment (cars and

CONVERTING IRON INTO STEEL
AT AN INDIANA FACTORY

trucks, aircraft of various kinds, ships and boats, railroad cars), and electrical equipment (television sets, computers, household appliances).

Every state has factories, large or small. But the group of states stretching from New York and New Jersey westward to Illinois and Wisconsin leads all other areas in manufacturing. These states have large centers of population, which supply workers as well as a rich market for manufactured goods. The areas surrounding the cities produce many of the raw materials used in manufacturing. And all these states have unusually good land and water transportation for bringing in raw materials and sending out finished goods.

Other states that rank high in manufacturing include California and Texas. They, too, have big cities, large supplies of raw materials, and good transportation.

Which States Claim Presidents?

Which state is called the "Mother of Presidents"?

VIRGINIA, because more Presidents of the United States have been born there than in any other state. These eight Presidents were born in Virginia (the number following each name tells which President the person was in numerical order):

George Washington, 1st
Thomas Jefferson, 3rd
James Madison, 4th
James Monroe, 5th

William Henry Harrison, 9th
John Tyler, 10th
Zachary Taylor, 12th
Woodrow Wilson, 28th

Which state ranks next in number of Presidents born in the state?

OHIO is a close second to Virginia, with these seven Presidents:

Ulysses S. Grant, 18th
Rutherford B. Hayes, 19th
James A. Garfield, 20th
Benjamin Harrison, 23rd

William McKinley, 25th
William Howard Taft, 27th
Warren G. Harding, 29th

Which state ranks third?

NEW YORK, which was the birthplace of these four Presidents:

Martin Van Buren, 8th
Millard Fillmore, 13th

Theodore Roosevelt, 26th
Franklin D. Roosevelt, 32nd

Which state is next?

MASSACHUSETTS, with three Presidents:

John Adams, 2nd
John Quincy Adams, 6th
John F. Kennedy, 35th

Which states have been the birthplace of two Presidents each?

NORTH CAROLINA:	James K. Polk, 11th
	Andrew Johnson, 17th
TEXAS:	Dwight D. Eisenhower, 34th
	Lyndon B. Johnson, 36th
VERMONT:	Chester A. Arthur, 21st
	Calvin Coolidge, 30th

Which states claim one President each?

CALIFORNIA:	Richard M. Nixon, 37th
GEORGIA:	Jimmy (James Earl) Carter, 39th
IOWA:	Herbert Hoover, 31st
KENTUCKY:	Abraham Lincoln, 16th
MISSOURI:	Harry S. Truman, 33rd
NEBRASKA:	Gerald R. Ford, 38th
NEW HAMPSHIRE:	Franklin Pierce, 14th
NEW JERSEY:	Grover Cleveland, 22nd and 24th
PENNSYLVANIA:	James Buchanan, 15th
SOUTH CAROLINA:	Andrew Jackson, 7th *

* Andrew Jackson was born in Waxhaw, a backwoods settlement on the border between South Carolina and North Carolina, and both states claim the site of the settlement. President Jackson himself considered South Carolina to be his birthplace.

Which States
Claim Vice-Presidents?

As a birthplace of Vice-Presidents of the United States, New York is the leader by far, with eight. Kentucky is next, followed by Ohio and Vermont.

In the following list, the number after the name tells which Vice-President the person was in numerical order. The name of the person who was President at the time is shown in parentheses.

CALIFORNIA:	Richard M. Nixon, 36th (Eisenhower)
INDIANA:	Thomas R. Marshall, 28th (Wilson)
IOWA:	Henry A. Wallace, 33rd (F. D. Roosevelt)
KANSAS:	Charles Curtis, 31st (Hoover)
KENTUCKY:	Richard M. Johnson, 9th (Van Buren)
	John C. Breckinridge, 14th (Buchanan)
	Adlai E. Stevenson, 23rd (Cleveland)
	Alben W. Barkley, 35th (Truman)
MAINE:	Hannibal Hamlin, 15th (Lincoln)
	Nelson A. Rockefeller, 41st (Ford)
MARYLAND:	Spiro T. Agnew, 39th (Nixon)
MASSACHUSETTS:	John Adams, 1st (Washington)
	Elbridge Gerry, 5th (Madison)
MINNESOTA:	Walter F. Mondale, 42nd (Carter)
MISSOURI:	Harry S. Truman, 34th (F. D. Roosevelt)
NEBRASKA:	Gerald R. Ford, 40th (Nixon)
NEW HAMPSHIRE:	Henry Wilson, 18th (Grant)
NEW JERSEY:	Aaron Burr, 3rd (Jefferson)
	Garret A. Hobart, 24th (McKinley)

NEW YORK:	George Clinton, 4th (Jefferson and Madison)
	Daniel D. Tompkins, 6th (Monroe)
	Martin Van Buren, 8th (Jackson)
	Millard Fillmore, 12th (Taylor)
	Schuyler Colfax, 17th (Grant)
	William A. Wheeler, 19th (Hayes)
	Theodore Roosevelt, 25th (McKinley)
	James S. Sherman, 27th (Taft)
NORTH CAROLINA:	William R. King, 13th (Pierce)
	Andrew Johnson, 16th (Lincoln)
OHIO:	Thomas A. Hendricks, 21st (Cleveland)
	Charles W. Fairbanks, 26th (T. Roosevelt)
	Charles G. Dawes, 30th (Coolidge)
PENNSYLVANIA:	George M. Dallas, 11th (Polk)
SOUTH CAROLINA:	John C. Calhoun, 7th (John Q. Adams and Andrew Jackson)
SOUTH DAKOTA:	Hubert H. Humphrey, 38th (L. B. Johnson)
TEXAS:	John N. Garner, 32nd (F. D. Roosevelt)
	Lyndon B. Johnson, 37th (Kennedy)
VERMONT:	Chester A. Arthur, 20th (Garfield)
	Levi P. Morton, 22nd (B. Harrison)
	Calvin Coolidge, 29th (Harding)
VIRGINIA:	Thomas Jefferson, 2nd (John Adams)
	John Tyler, 10th (W. H. Harrison)

What's in a Nickname?

Who's a Hoosier?

A Hoosier is an Indianan. This is the nickname of both the state and the people. No one knows exactly where this name came from or how Indiana acquired it, but it is one of the best known and best loved of all the state nicknames.

Which state is the Show-Me State?

That's Missouri. Although no one knows the exact origin of this nickname, either, almost everyone knows the saying, "I'm from Missouri, and you'll have to show me."

Why is Colorado called the Centennial State?

This nickname comes from the fact that Colorado became a state in 1876—the centennial (100th anniversary) of the signing of the Declaration of Independence.

Who are Sooners?

They are Oklahomans, and the state is called the Sooner State. This nickname comes from the time (April 22, 1889) when a small amount of land in Oklahoma, then called Indian Territory, was first opened to settlers. People who wanted to claim land were supposed to line up at the border, await the opening signal, and then rush in to stake their claims. But some people had found ways to locate desirable land in advance, and they were able to stake their claims "sooner" than the others. They were called "Sooners," and from them the state and the people of Oklahoma acquired a nickname.

Who are Tarheels?

The people of North Carolina have this nickname, and the state is called the Tarheel State. Tar once was an important product of North Carolina's vast pine forests, but the exact origin of the nickname is uncertain. One story of the origin goes back to the time of the Civil War, 1861–1865, when there was talk of putting tar on the heels of some soldiers to make them stick better in battle.

Which state is the Volunteer State?

Tennessee proudly bears this nickname. Soldiers from Tennessee, led by Andrew Jackson, played an important part in the War of 1812. Later, during the Mexican War (1846–1848), many Tennesseans offered their services. All these volunteers helped give the state its nickname.

Why is Kentucky called the Bluegrass State?

Kentucky is famous for a kind of grass called bluegrass. It is not really blue, but it has a bluish tinge when it is in full bloom. Some of the world's best-known racehorses have grazed on its bluegrass pastures.

Which state is the Granite State?

New Hampshire has this nickname, which comes from the fine building granite quarried in the state.

. . . and the Equality State?

Wyoming well deserves this nickname because in 1869 the Wyoming territorial legislature gave women equal rights with men to vote and hold public office. These rights were included in the state constitution of 1890, making Wyoming the first state to give women the vote.

All the other states have nicknames, too. Some have more than one, and some have had several during their histories. The present nicknames of the rest of states are given in the following list. Many of these are official—that is, they have been adopted by acts of the state legislatures.

ALABAMA: Heart of Dixie
ALASKA: The Great Land
ARIZONA: Grand Canyon State
ARKANSAS: Land of Opportunity
CALIFORNIA: Golden State
CONNECTICUT: Constitution State
DELAWARE: First State; Diamond State
FLORIDA: Sunshine State
GEORGIA: Empire State of the South; Peach State
HAWAII: Aloha State
IDAHO: Gem State
ILLINOIS: Land of Lincoln; Prairie State
IOWA: Hawkeye State
KANSAS: Sunflower State
LOUISIANA: Pelican State
MAINE: Pine Tree State
MARYLAND: Old Line State
MASSACHUSETTS: Bay State
MICHIGAN: Wolverine State; Water–Winter Wonderland
MINNESOTA: North Star State; Gopher State
MISSISSIPPI: Magnolia State
MONTANA: Treasure State
NEBRASKA: Cornhusker State
NEVADA: Silver State
NEW JERSEY: Garden State
NEW MEXICO: Land of Enchantment
NEW YORK: Empire State
NORTH DAKOTA: Flickertail State; Sioux State
OHIO: Buckeye State
OREGON: Beaver State; Sunset State
PENNSYLVANIA: Keystone State
RHODE ISLAND: Little Rhody
SOUTH CAROLINA: Palmetto State
SOUTH DAKOTA: Coyote State; Sunshine State
TEXAS: Lone Star State
UTAH: Beehive State
VERMONT: Green Mountain State
VIRGINIA: Old Dominion
WASHINGTON: Evergreen State
WEST VIRGINIA: Mountain State
WISCONSIN: Badger State

The States and Their Capitals— a List

Here are lists that you can use to test yourself or someone else on naming the state capitals. It you are testing yourself, cover the capitals with a strip of paper.

STATE	CAPITAL
1. ALABAMA	1. MONTGOMERY
2. ALASKA	2. JUNEAU
3. ARIZONA	3. PHOENIX
4. ARKANSAS	4. LITTLE ROCK
5. CALIFORNIA	5. SACRAMENTO
6. COLORADO	6. DENVER
7. CONNECTICUT	7. HARTFORD
8. DELAWARE	8. DOVER
9. FLORIDA	9. TALLAHASSEE
10. GEORGIA	10. ATLANTA
11. HAWAII	11. HONOLULU
12. IDAHO	12. BOISE
13. ILLINOIS	13. SPRINGFIELD
14. INDIANA	14. INDIANAPOLIS
15. IOWA	15. DES MOINES
16. KANSAS	16. TOPEKA
17. KENTUCKY	17. FRANKFORT
18. LOUISIANA	18. BATON ROUGE
19. MAINE	19. AUGUSTA
20. MARYLAND	20. ANNAPOLIS
21. MASSACHUSETTS	21. BOSTON
22. MICHIGAN	22. LANSING
23. MINNESOTA	23. SAINT PAUL
24. MISSISSIPPI	24. JACKSON
25. MISSOURI	25. JEFFERSON CITY

STATE	CAPITAL
26. MONTANA	26. HELENA
27. NEBRASKA	27. LINCOLN
28. NEVADA	28. CARSON CITY
29. NEW HAMPSHIRE	29. CONCORD
30. NEW JERSEY	30. TRENTON
31. NEW MEXICO	31. SANTA FE
32. NEW YORK	32. ALBANY
33. NORTH CAROLINA	33. RALEIGH
34. NORTH DAKOTA	34. BISMARCK
35. OHIO	35. COLUMBUS
36. OKLAHOMA	36. OKLAHOMA CITY
37. OREGON	37. SALEM
38. PENNSYLVANIA	38. HARRISBURG
39. RHODE ISLAND	39. PROVIDENCE
40. SOUTH CAROLINA	40. COLUMBIA
41. SOUTH DAKOTA	41. PIERRE
42. TENNESSEE	42. NASHVILLE
43. TEXAS	43. AUSTIN
44. UTAH	44. SALT LAKE CITY
45. VERMONT	45. MONTPELIER
46. VIRGINIA	46. RICHMOND
47. WASHINGTON	47. OLYMPIA
48. WEST VIRGINIA	48. CHARLESTON
49. WISCONSIN	49. MADISON
50. WYOMING	50. CHEYENNE

The Emblems of the States

Why do the states have flags, seals, mottoes, birds, flowers, trees, and other emblems? *

One definition of the word "state" is "a body of people politically organized and occupying a certain territory." We can see how this definition applies to a state of the United States. A state, first of all, must have people. Then the people must have a certain area of land that they call their own, and they must have a government under which they live.

One of the first things that the founders (the people who help to establish, or found, a state) do is to choose a name for the state. The name establishes the identity of the state and helps to give it a "personality."

Then the founders have a flag made, using colors and designs that have a special meaning for the state. The flag becomes the main emblem of the state. Usually the founders choose a motto—a word, phrase, or sentence (often in Latin) that helps express the "character" of the state and gives the people a principle, or important idea, to guide their lives.

---

* It would take many pages to show and explain the details of all the flags and seals of the fifty states. The design of almost every one makes an interesting story that tells much about the history and the traditions of the state. The articles on the states in *The New Book of Knowledge* and some other encyclopedias give information about the state emblems. Too, most states have special leaflets or booklets showing and explaining their emblems. These can be obtained by writing to the secretary of state in each state.

The founders usually give careful thought to the design of at least one other emblem—the state seal, often called the "great seal." The seal becomes the "signature" of the state, and it is placed on all official documents. Most of the states have their motto on the state seal.

Each state also has a bird, flower, tree, and maybe other emblems that help express the personality of the state and tell something important or unusual about it. Sometimes these are chosen early in the life of the state, and sometimes they are selected later.

Most of the emblems are official—that is, they have been adopted by acts of the state legislature. In many instances, the schoolchildren of a state have helped to choose the bird, flower, or tree.

The state birds, flowers, and trees are listed on pages 62 — 63. Here are some questions that show how interesting a study of state emblems can be:

Which states have a horse as their state animal?
     The Morgan horse is the state animal of Vermont. (The story of the famous Morgan horse is told in the book *Justin Morgan Had a Horse,* by Marguerite Henry.) The Appaloosa is the state horse of Idaho.

Which states have a dog?
     Maryland has the Chesapeake Bay retriever as its state animal. Pennsylvania has the Great Dane, and Virginia, the American foxhound.

What are some of the other state animals?

California: grizzly bear
Colorado: bighorn sheep
Connecticut: sperm whale
Kansas: buffalo (bison)
New Mexico: black bear
Nevada: bighorn sheep

Oregon: beaver
Pennsylvania: white-tailed deer
South Dakota: coyote
Tennessee: raccoon
Wisconsin: badger

What are some of the state fish?

Alabama: tarpon
Alaska: king salmon
Maryland: striped bass

Massachusetts: cod
Michigan: trout
New Mexico: cutthroat trout

Which state has a breed of poultry as its state bird?

Rhode Island's state bird is the Rhode Island Red, a breed of poultry developed in the state and known all over the country.

Which state has a goose as its state bird?

The state bird of Hawaii is the nene, or Hawaiian goose.

What is unusual about Delaware's state bird?

The story of Delaware's state bird, the blue hen chicken, goes back to Revolutionary War times. It is said that when a company of Delaware men went off to war, they took with them game chickens (fighting cocks) that were of the brood of a famous blue hen. When the men were not in battle, they entertained themselves by holding cockfights. When they were in battle, they fought so well that they were compared to their fighting cocks, and they gained the nickname "Blue Hen's Chickens." Later, Delaware adopted the blue hen chicken as its state bird.

STATE	BIRD	FLOWER	TREE
Alabama	Yellowhammer	Camellia	Longleaf pine
Alaska	Willow ptarmigan	Forget-me-not	Sitka spruce
Arizona	Cactus wren	Saguaro cactus blossom	Paloverde
Arkansas	Mockingbird	Apple blossom	Shortleaf pine
California	California valley quail	Golden poppy	California redwood
Colorado	Lark bunting	Rocky Mountain columbine	Colorado blue spruce
Connecticut	American robin	Mountain laurel	White oak
Delaware	Blue hen chicken	Peach blossom	American holly
Florida	Mockingbird	Orange blossom	Cabbage palmetto
Georgia	Brown thrasher	Cherokee rose	Live oak
Hawaii	Nene (Hawaiian goose)	Red hibiscus	Kukui (candlenut tree)
Idaho	Mountain bluebird	Syringa	Western white pine
Illinois	Eastern cardinal	Meadow violet	Bur oak
Indiana	Cardinal	Peony	Tulip tree
Iowa	Eastern goldfinch	Wild rose	Oak
Kansas	Western meadowlark	Sunflower	Cottonwood
Kentucky	Cardinal	Goldenrod	Kentucky coffee tree
Louisiana	Eastern brown pelican	Magnolia	Bald cypress
Maine	Chickadee	Eastern white pine cone and tassel	Eastern white pine
Maryland	Baltimore oriole	Black-eyed Susan	White oak
Massachusetts	Chickadee	Mayflower	American elm
Michigan	Robin	Apple blossom	Eastern white pine
Minnesota	Loon	Showy (pink-and-white) lady's slipper	Red (Norway) pine

STATE	BIRD	FLOWER	TREE
Mississippi	Mockingbird	Magnolia blossom	Southern magnolia
Missouri	Bluebird	Hawthorn	Flowering dogwood
Montana	Western meadowlark	Bitterroot	Ponderosa pine
Nebraska	Western meadowlark	Goldenrod	Cottonwood
Nevada	Mountain bluebird	Sagebrush	Single-leaf pinyon
New Hampshire	Purple finch	Purple lilac	Paper birch
New Jersey	Eastern goldfinch	Purple violet	Red oak
New Mexico	Roadrunner	Yucca	Pinyon
New York	Bluebird (not official)	Rose	Sugar maple
North Carolina	Cardinal	Dogwood	Pine
North Dakota	Western meadowlark	Wild prairie rose	American elm
Ohio	Cardinal	Scarlet carnation	Ohio buckeye
Oklahoma	Scissor-tailed flycatcher	Mistletoe	Redbud
Oregon	Western meadowlark	Oregon grape	Douglas fir
Pennsylvania	Ruffed grouse	Mountain laurel	Eastern hemlock
Rhode Island	Rhode Island Red	Violet	Red maple
South Carolina	Carolina wren	Yellow jasmine	Palmetto
South Dakota	Ring-necked pheasant	Pasqueflower	White spruce
Tennessee	Mockingbird	Iris	Yellow poplar
Texas	Mockingbird	Bluebonnet	Pecan
Utah	Sea gull	Sego lily	Blue spruce
Vermont	Hermit thrush	Red clover	Sugar maple
Virginia	Cardinal	Flowering dogwood	Dogwood (not official)
Washington	Willow goldfinch	Coast rhododendron	Western hemlock
West Virginia	Cardinal	Great rhododendron	Sugar maple
Wisconsin	Robin	Violet	Sugar maple
Wyoming	Western meadowlark	Indian paintbrush	Cottonwood

Index